Apple

Orange

Mango

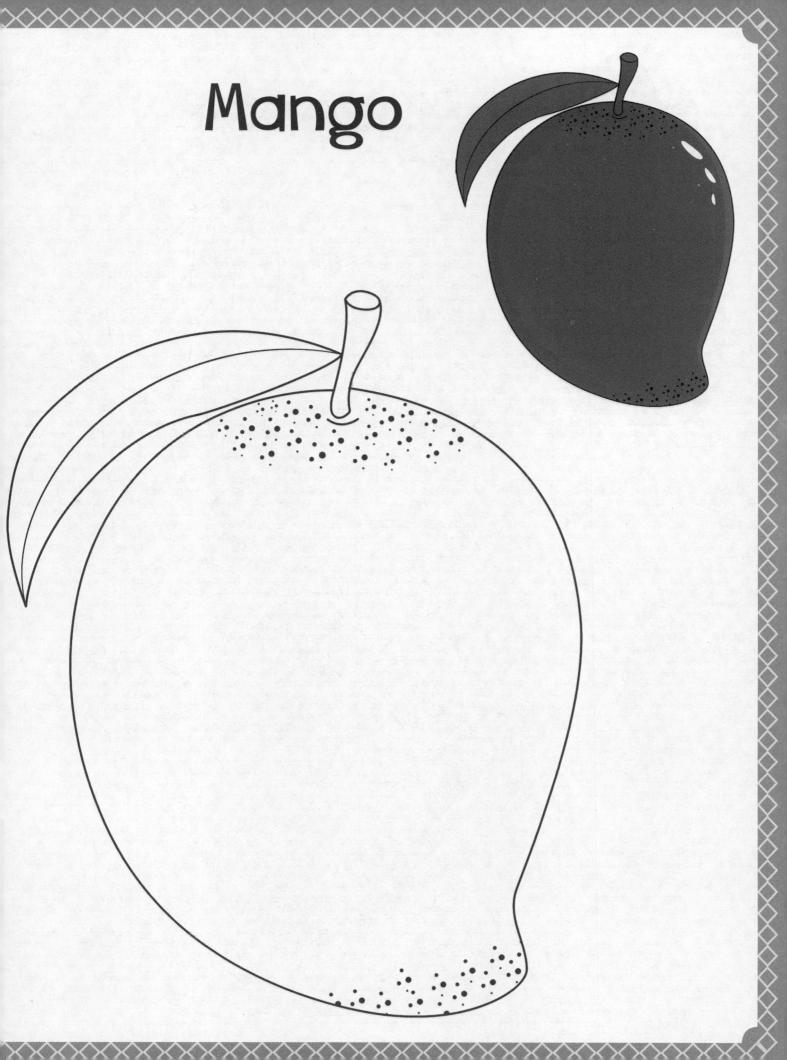

Pineapple

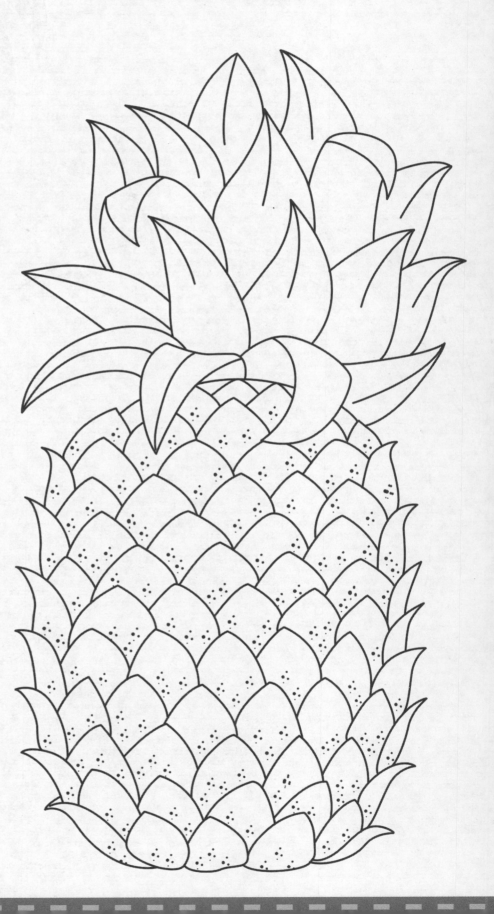

Pear

Strawberry

Cherry

Pomegranate

Peach

Grapes

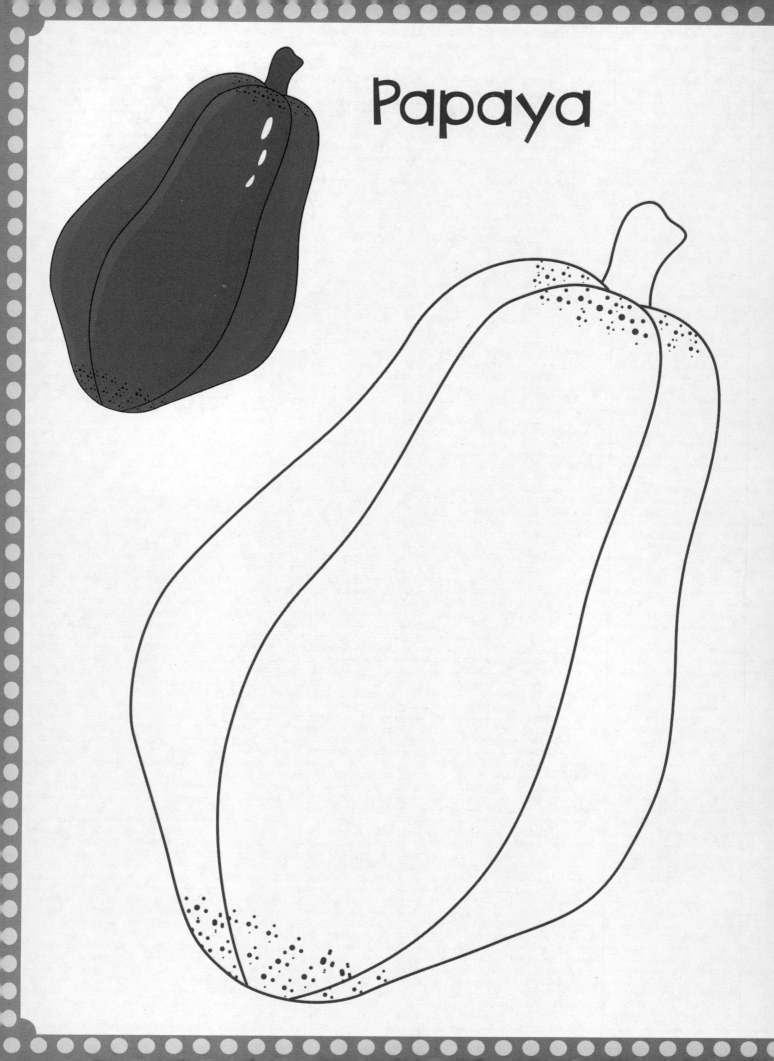

Papaya

Elephant

Lion

Hippopotamus

Giraffe

Monkey

Panda

Kangaroo

Bear

Fox

Cheetah

Rhinoceros

Wolf

Tiger

Koala

Deer

Kingfisher

Kiwi

Pigeon

Sparrow

Hornbill

Turkey

Owl

Parrot

Peacock

Woodpecker

Eagle

Dinosaur

Rabbit

Guinea Pig

Horse

Cow

Cat

Dog

Butterfly

Dragonfly

Bug

Caterpillar

Ant

Slug

Crab

Octopus

Crocodile

Lobster

Oyster

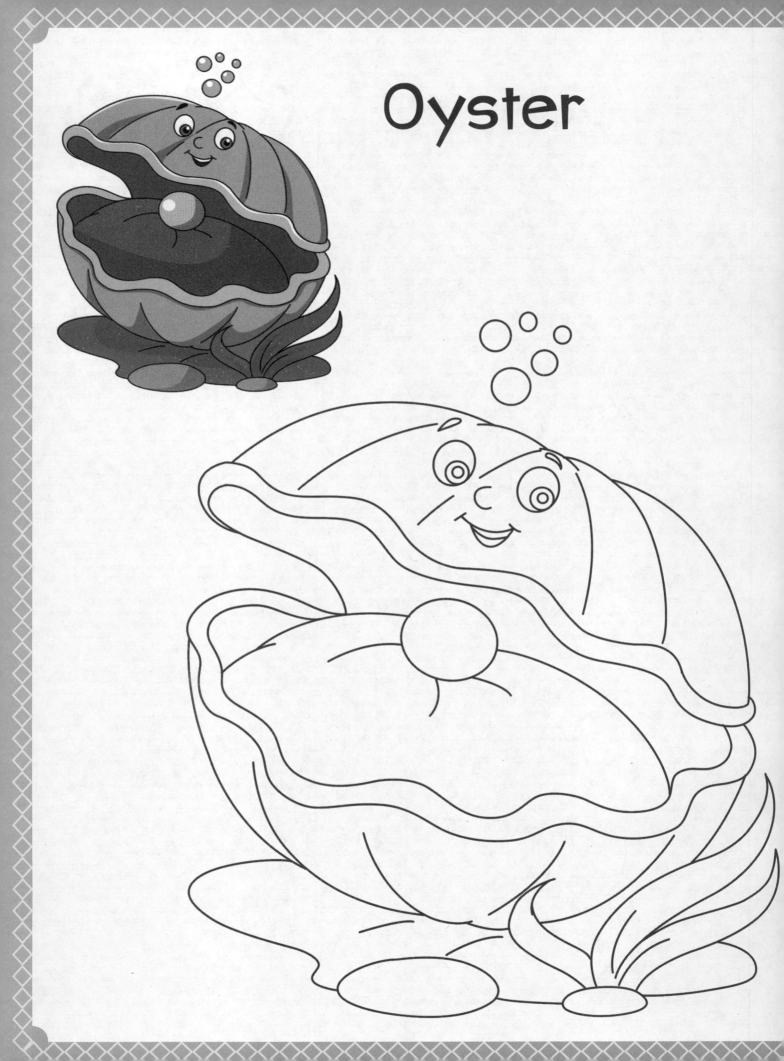

Sea Horse

Shark

Angelfish

Goldfish

Blue Whale

Porcupinefish

Clownfish

Starfish

Sea Turtle

Bus

Car

Motorbike

Ambulance

Aeroplane

Helicopter

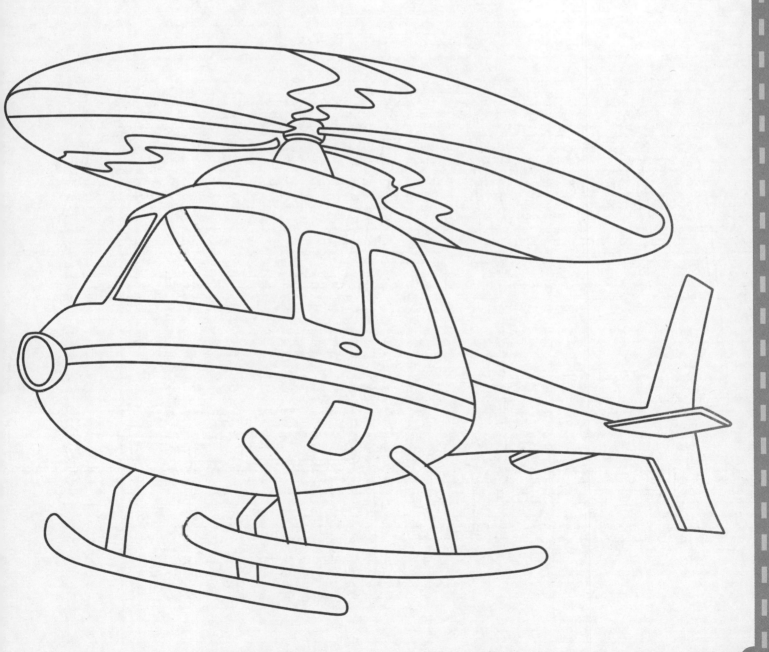

Van

Train

Tractor

Truck

Ship

Submarine

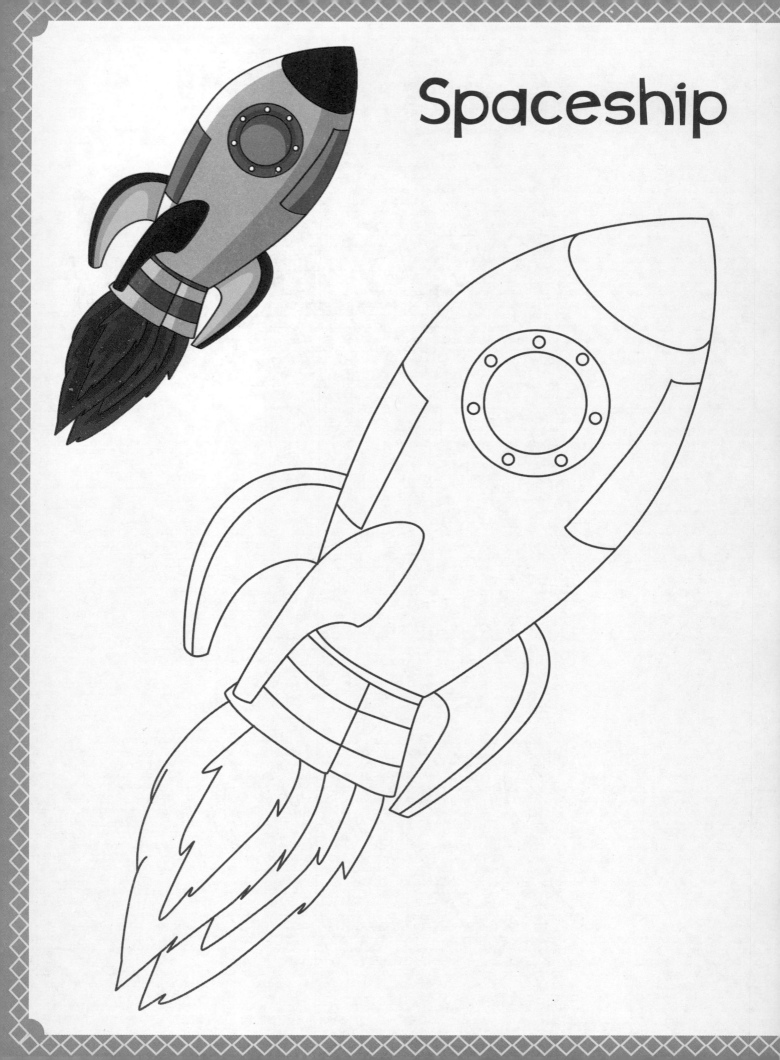

Spaceship

Cricket

Boxing

Cycling

Ice Hockey

Baseball

Tennis

Swimming

Golf

Archery

Running

Carpenter

Chef

Butler

Pilot

Policeman

Doctor

Firefighter

Teacher

Artist

Engineer

Actor

Clown

Singer

Archaeologist

Can you find the two differences between these two bears?

Can you spot two differences between these two pictures of a pirate boy?

4

Do you see two identical cars or can you find two differences?

Can you spot the two differences between these two snowmen?

Are they the same chef, or can you spot two differences?

Can you spot two differences between the two birds?

Can you find the two differences between these two policewomen?

Can you spot the two differences between these two mice?

Are they the same little girl, or can you spot two differences?

These two teddy bears look identical. Can you find three differences?

12

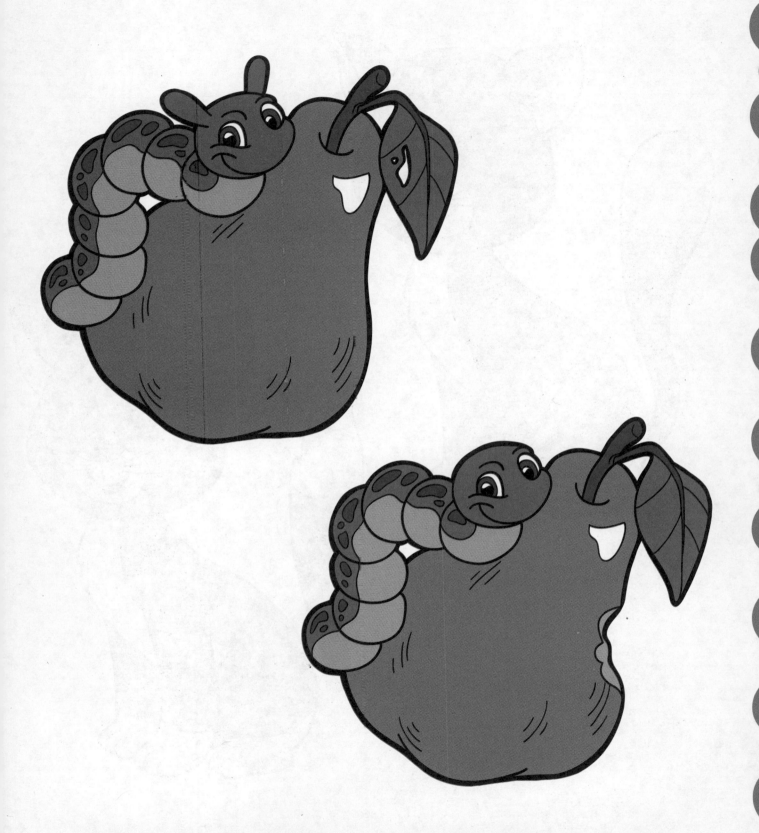

Can you spot three differences between these two pictures of a worm on a pear?

Can you find the three differences between these two cute tigers?

Can you spot the three differences between these two penguins on a sledge?

Can you spot three differences between these two shy bees?

Are these two hedgehogs identical, or can you find three differences?

Can you find three differences between these two vixens?

Can you spot the three differences between these two dogs?

There are three differences between these adorable penguins. Can you find them?

Can you spot three differences between these two snails?

Can you spot the four differences between these two wise owls?

Are these two happy puppies exactly the same, or can you spot four differences?

Mark the four differences between these two reindeers.

Spot four differences between these playful kittens.

Can you spot four differences between the two birds?

Can you spot four differences between these two fishes?

Are these turtles identical, or can you spot four differences?

Mark the four differences between these little lambs.

Can you spot the four differences between these two huge dogs?

Are these two bear cubs and their honey pots exactly the same, or can you find four differences?

Can you spot five differences between these two studious tigers?

Can you spot five differences between these two bunnies?

Can you spot five differences between these two artistic elephants?

Can you find five differences between these two elegant poodles?

Can you spot five differences between these two antique clocks?

Are these potted plants exactly the same, or can you find five differences?

Can you spot the five differences between these two delicious cupcakes?

Can you find five differences between these two bouquets of flowers?

Are they identical airplanes, or can you find five differences?

Can you spot five differences between these two happy elephants?

Mark the six differences between these two pictures of a father and son with their cars.

Can you find six differences between these two happy group photos?

Can you find all six differences between these two pictures of academic turtles?

Can you spot six differences between these two pictures of turtles at school?

Can you find all six differences between these two packs of dogs?

Can you spot all six differences between these two goofy group photos?

Both pictures look identical. However, can you spot six differences between them?

Can you spot six differences between these two picnic scenes?

Mark six differences between these two pictures of children playing in the park.

Can you spot all seven differences between these two pictures of hares?

Can you spot all seven differences between these two jungle scenes?

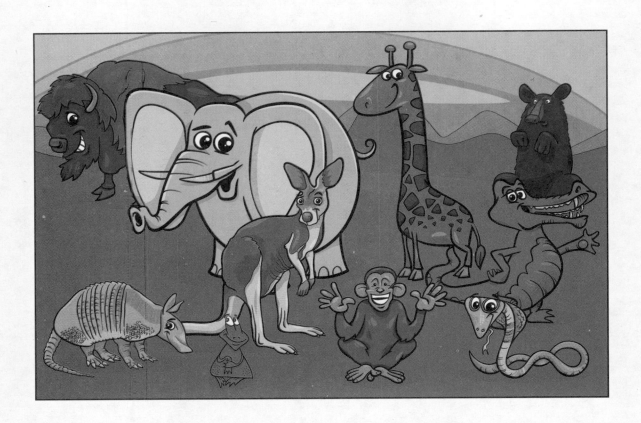

Are these two images of wild animals exactly the same, or can you find seven differences?

Can you find seven differences between these two drawings of wild animals?

54

Are these robots from the future exactly the same, or can you spot seven differences?

Can you spot seven differences between these two pictures of best friends?

These two pictures of kids at a costume party look identical. However, can you spot seven differences?

Can you spot seven differences between these two shoals of colorful fishes?

Can you find seven differences between these two pictures of kids in the park?

Can you find seven differences between these two goofy pictures of wild animals?

Can you find seven differences between these two spooky Halloween scenes?

Can you spot eight differences between these two images of a camel in the desert?

Can you spot eight differences between these two groups of friends?

Can you spot eight differences between these two images of recharging robots?

Can you spot all eight differences between these two pictures of happy kids in a school bus?

Can you find all eight differences between these two pictures of birds posing?

Can you spot eight differences between these two pictures of the clowns?

Can you spot all eight differences between these two circus shows?

Mark the eight differences between these two images of a pirate crew.

Can you spot eight differences between the two images of kids playing in the park?

Can you find eight differences between these two cheesy pictures of mice?

Can you find nine differences between these two near-identical images of birds in a tree?

Can you spot all nine differences between these two farm scenes?

Mark all nine differences between these two pictures of children playing in the park.

Can you spot all nine differences between these two spooky pictures?

Are they identical pictures of dramatic animals, or can you spot nine differences?

Mark all nine differences between these two drawings of office-going dogs.

Can you spot nine differences between these two pictures of naughty children flying a kite?

Are these two drawings of little chefs identical, or can you find nine differences?

These two pictures of kids catching butterflies look identical. However can you spot nine differences?

Can you find all nine differences between these two drawings of a fox and a boy in the wilderness?

Mark all ten differences between these two images of the committee of animals and birds.

Can you find the ten differences between these two pictures of marine animals?

Can you spot the ten differences between these two pictures of plants growing in a desert?

84

Can you spot the ten differences between these two pictures of a bird in a lake?

Is it the same group of aliens, or can you spot ten differences between the two pictures?

Mark the ten differences between the two pictures of dancing robots.

These two pictures of wild animals look identical.
However, can you find ten differences?

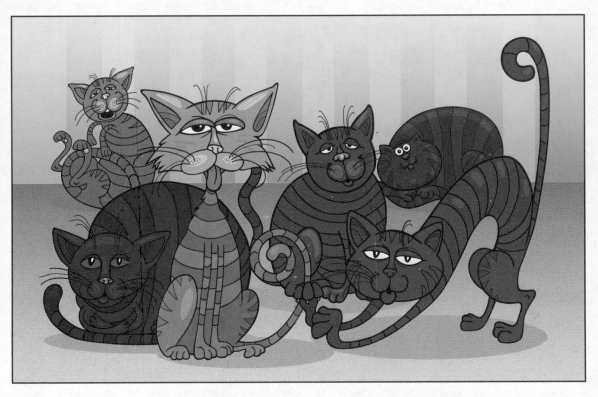

Can you spot ten differences between these pictures of goofy cats?

Are these two sceneries identical, or can you find eleven differences?

Are these prehistoric pictures identical, or can you spot eleven differences?

Can you spot all eleven differences between these two pictures of insects?

Can you find eleven differences between these two images of a tiny chick in an egg?

Can you spot all eleven differences between these two colorful pictures?

Can you find the eleven differences between these two pictures of animals in the wild?

Can you spot eleven differences between these two pictures of outer space?

Are these two pictures of a snorkeling cat identical, or can you spot eleven differences?

These two images of identical flocks of sheep have twelve hidden differences. Can you find them?

Can you spot all twelve differences between these two goofy groups of aliens?

Can you spot twelve differences between these two pictures of an angry ram running behind a man?

Can you find all twelve differences between these two images of birds singing in the garden?

Can you find all twelve differences between these two images of impending disaster?

Are these two pictures of pirates exactly the same, or can you spot twelve differences?

Can you find all twelve differences between these two snowy scenes?

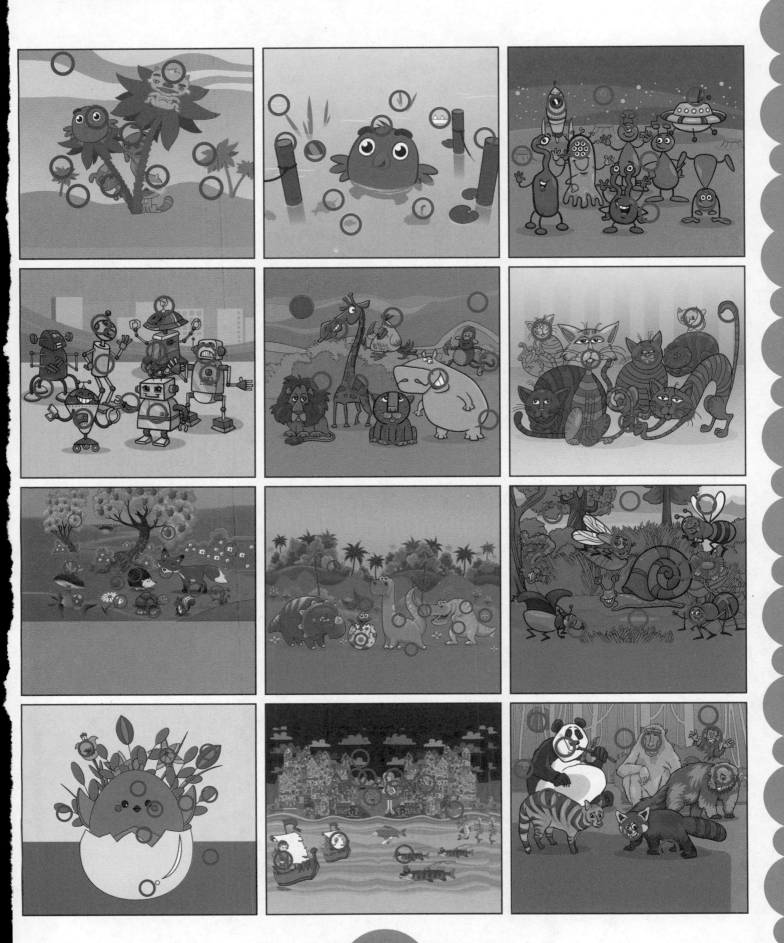